A NEW INDEX
FOR PREDICTING
CATASTROPHES

A NEW INDEX
FOR PREDICTING
CATASTROPHES

Poems

MADHUR ANAND

McCLELLAND & STEWART

Library and Archives Canada Cataloguing in Publication data available upon request

ISBN: 978-0-7710-0698-2
ebook ISBN: 978-0-7710-0699-9

Published simultaneously in the United States of America
by McClelland & Stewart, a division of Random House of Canada Limited,
a Penguin Random House Company.

Library of Congress Control Number: 2014920840

Typeset in Seria by M&S, Toronto
Printed and bound in USA

McClelland & Stewart,
a division of Random House of Canada Limited,
a Penguin Random House Company
www.penguinrandomhouse.ca

1 2 3 4 5   19 18 17 16 15

for my parents

O=C−H   1

H−C−OH   2

HO−C−H   3

H−C−OH   4

H−C−OH   5

CH_2OH 6

$_6CH_2OH$

1, 5 ether linkage

H C_5 O   OH

H

C_4 OH   H C_1

HO C_3 C_2 H

H   OH

D-glucose

Is it in the sun that truth begins?

ADRIENNE RICH

Everything existing in the universe is the fruit of chance and necessity.

DEMOCRITUS

CONTENTS

III. NO TWO THINGS CAN BE MORE EQUAL

IV. THE STRATEGY OF THE MAJORITY

What We Don't See
in Light's Dark Reactions

What We Don't See in Light's Dark Reactions

The rejection of reds, a gap of blues, chlorophyll
absorbing necessary wavelengths. The public good
of peacocks, feather primordia morphogenesis
behind the wheel. Function and shine of an evening
brooch, butterflied. Shiver and heat: sky-scraping violet,
Brazilian soccer shirts, and cachaça on ice. Bird
of paradise peering through closed canopy. Flowers,
like Heliconia, mistaken for flight. Fancy.
Economy. Monkeys and mycorrhizae playing
non-zero-sum games. Giant seed pods like maracas,
chandeliers dimmed, everything instrumental, quiet
breaths exchanged by the carbon pool. Oranges, crushed, too
easily spent. Green going underground. Tropical
bonds, shape-shifting mouths – nameless and innumerable –
moving iron-rich soil, liberating minerals
and death. Liana hanging. Black-green-red, a parting
of leaves. Something winged, ringed molecules, sugar from light.

Cantharellus

We were boring jack pines, storing their cores in plastic
drinking straws. It had been raining. I'm no naturalist
but understand the association of fungi
and forests, their partiality for recent rain.
I don't know birds or bark, but once grasped indifference
by the neck. Such that when I saw them – creamy orange
against first brown, then grey, then green – I was 95
per cent sure. I brushed aside soil, lichen, moss, placed them
into yellow hard hats. Later we would discern which
tree rings were false. Of greater concern was my own
mortality. And mushrooms I decided were true.

Wild populations recognize that the linearity,
the relative rareness, the major museums, or any area
which is known, is a surrogate
for proximity

Stream beetles, Galapagos finches, and Israeli
passerine birds are transformed
into an index of limited
available information

Elytral lengths, slope of the regression,
and mid-latitude precipitation
unravel the anomalies

A prolonged change is also under scrutiny

J. Babin-Fenske, M. Anand, and Y. Alarie, "Rapid Morphological Change
in Stream Beetle Museum Specimens Correlates with Climate Change,"
Ecological Entomology 33, no. 5 (2008): 646–51.

Cosmos bipinnatus

Imminent is always less than desirable. Ice
white, boldly bordered, splashed or stippled. We've been letting

the ivy go for how long? Nostalgia for the turn
of a century, nest at the top of a TV

antenna tower, which could be integral, could be
squirrels. Four parts water to one part sugar feeds the

hum. Now we curtain, now we dream of iron blackbirds.
Place seeds like black clipped fingernails from last year's packet

of Cosmos 'Candy Stripe' in egg cartons reclaimed from
the blue box. A dozen divided by four, six, twelve.

Occasionally a pure crimson bloom may appear.

BETULA PAPYRIFERA

Something native, sequenced, compiled, dying to be recalled.
White encoded with black dots and vascular dashes
from the rented cottage on Ahmic Lake to plastic
bags in our hatchback. I stole a branch the length of two
phone books. Gorgeous and genuine against the living
room pine shelves, its bark hospitable to pale crustose
lichen and first-century Buddhists writing down how
to survive: await the ringtones of light and moisture,
length inversely proportional to the frequency
of occurrence, on–off clicks directly understood.

THE SIMPLEST SIGNIFICANT VIRUS

That wishbone you pulled from my pharynx when I was three.
I type polio to a world that barely contains
you. I discover the soccer ball symmetry of
the particle, its short and simple genome. Then I
type in your common name. Find a photo of handsome
you: "In dark suit sitting at desk. Copyright status
unknown." It's true our family name means joy and I've spread
it, an invasion populating the middle names
and Saturday morning fields of my own two children.
There's no escaping it. That, and the resemblance of
my temper, the bridge of my nose, to yours. Sometimes I
think the "sweet-like-honey joy" that is my full name, my
trophy-laden life, will sum up to the atrophied
muscle of your little boy leg, but it won't equate.

VACCINIUM ANGUSTIFOLIUM

Lowbush law or just light's kindness, slightly acidic
hills exhale to fruition tiny crowned spheres. Thin red
liquid is clear but wrong. Their berries are alas false
accessory fruit, flesh from the surface of petals.
What's beneath becomes second nature. Geometry
of rhizomes, dirt, gossip, antioxidants, memory.
Come July, ripe museum hours, the dead-on pigments,
Rayleigh scattering. When every non-fiction begins
to factor in the predictive power of petals.
Pale white lampshades, designed to keep all the good light in.

PINK CYCLAMEN, *THE ECONOMIST*, BEIJING AIRPORT

My attention is drawn to the vulva understory
of a palm in a plastic planter. Upswept petals
rooted in black, aerated by Styrofoam-white balls.
In the Mediterranean, tubers lie dormant
every summer and seeds only germinate in
limestone crevices. I flip lip glosses, wristwatches,
awaiting flight. Time is a latent variable.
To become endangered by scanty dispersal skills
or eye candy blessed by Adam Smith's invisible hand.
Everywhere markets scream in sans serif. I carry on.

There's a new index for predicting catastrophes.
It's the decreasing rate of recovery from small
perturbations. The critical slowing down before
a tipping point. Like taking a picture when I leave
out the wire fence and then move in for a close-up
of the Brangus cow standing right behind it. I'm taught
she's been bred for her disease resistance, tolerance
to heat, and outstanding maternal instincts. I look
for the three-eighths Brahman, traces of shared ancestry.
It's autumn. I've flown to Texas to meet my future
father-in-law. The vistas are simple and golden.
But then this brown cow appears, stands too still, becomes time,
consuming. That's when I see signs: she's just given birth.

The Chipping and the Tree

Spizella passerina, Spizella arborea

Songbirds of Peterson's guide defy fragility.
They live on top shelves with defined range maps, Latin names.
They are ideal, forever in caps, black or rufous
eyeliner. They don't fall apart by lost interest,
pollen, burnt meteorites, saltation of cornfields.

◯

In the Bible, two turtledoves can be sacrificed
to enter the house of God, two sparrows are sold for
a penny, and the black hairs on my head are numbered.
I'm trying to comprehend economy. The law
of diminishing returns dictates it's worth knowing.

◯

Chipping sparrow's haplotype depth is more akin to
red-winged blackbird's than to song sparrow's. *Passer* is of
Least Concern. The backyard sparrows share ancestors with
Tyrannosaurus, but the American Tree is
phylogenetically distant, visits in winter.

○

The low-pitched call of two glass doves the dimensions of
bee hummingbirds claim I'm a thief. That I stole them from
Mrs. Williamson's living room when I was eight,
had been taught long division and should have known better.
I knew and didn't. The simplest flight call being: *seen?*

○

The truth? I saw them, touched them, enclosed them in my hand.

THREE LAWS OF ECONOMICS

There's a dead space between mouth and lung. It's the volume
of inhaled air that does not take part in gas exchange.
Benefits can accrue. For example, inflation.

⬡

I hate balloons, the tentative permanence of air,
the conceit (I'm made from a tree!), the shock when they burst.
Fractal tears. Random shreds. Hurried externality.

⬡

The shots began today. Birch and ragweed in one arm.
Cat and dog in the other. In a few years you might
attain immunity. Chances of success compound.

Suede

But if salt has lost its taste, how shall its saltiness be restored?
– Matthew 5:13

At the age of thirteen I took my First Communion and slipped
the round white wafer into my back pocket. I was used to being
handed raisins and almonds at a temple where the only English
was "the truth always prevails."

My best friend witnessed it,
said nothing, had tested my faith many times down by the ravine
where some teen had gone missing that summer as if she
had lost her host. As if it were an honest mistake. I was innocent

but not without sin. I hid my voice. I did not ask good questions.
I hid my light. The thing itself felt like Styrofoam, inconclusive
as an unused condom, but with even less intention.

I threw it out

in the upstairs bathroom, the one with the powder-blue double sink.
I buried it under toilet paper rolls, a crushed Dove box, used
maxi-pads my mother would, without a word, make disappear.

I am vain and guilty of overcompensation. I once saw quilted
wheat fields in Saskatchewan spring and shouted: My God, fuck me.
Even now strangers may watch me watching myself in my new

honey-suede boots. In someone's eyes I was too young, it could
have been porn. But I am thankful, for my voice has gotten sweeter
with age. I know what it means, dear God, to melt on my tongue.

WE'RE NOT WORRIED

Danish astronomers have just discovered sugar

– simple molecules of glycolaldehyde – floating
in the gas around a young, sun-like star, four hundred
light years away. The molecules are falling
                                        toward
a binary star, a system of two bodies,
                                        one
primary, one companion, orbiting about
a common centre of mass. This space sugar, they think,
helps replicate DNA. We too orbit. Tonight

it's ice cream at The Boathouse Tea Room, noticing where
the Speed River's melting and, more urgently, the sides
of cones. We choose chocolate and vanilla, measure
the deviations. An old lady is feeding geese.

Astronauts wanted neapolitan for their trips
to the moon. Freeze-dried prototypes proved impractical.
Crumbs were dangerous to microgravity, like bird

parts in plane engines. Now they sell it at the NASA
gift shop, so we can all travel to outer space too.

There are more choices than stars. Scientists are making
breakthroughs in slowing down melt, though can't make it healthy.

You can't take sugar out because of the role it plays
The chemical structure girds against dismantlement

SOLE AND PLAICE (ON THE MATHEMATICS OF FLATFISH)

Ss and Ps, graphic displays of dashed curves, effort
versus catch, fewer exponents when I cancel out
the redundant variables, the new addition
to the house, dinner reservations in Toronto.
I've been trying to have it all, make a good model.

In Paris, the Tour Eiffel traded off for a pond,
toy boats, an attraction of water and gravity.
Yellow Line 1, direction La Défense, the leading
end with no one driving, excited to be the first
to detect approaching light. Some graphs are so complex

they lie in between dimensions. The divine bistro
beside the cemetery that served *sole meunière*,
dredged in flour, then fried in butter, clarified by
heat and *je ne sais quoi*. It's everything I wanted.
And I said there must be a way to remove the bones
all in one go. Every spine, rib, and pin. Pulled like this.

Various Authors Have Described

architectural novelty
taxa including plants, insects, fishes, and birds
parental behaviour
an analogue for fitness
pots put outside into containers
exposed, temporary, and irregular offspring
seasonally and permanently difficult to determine habitats
southern France in autumn
longevity of the individual
a marsh
depth to be an absolute constraint
a constant probability of death
a string of arbitrarily bad years
a genetic component
the adaptive value of spring
potential nonlinearities
geese
a relationship broad enough to be meaningfully different

A. Charpentier, M. Anand, and C.T. Bauch, "Variable Offspring Size as an
Adaptation to Environmental Heterogeneity in a Clonal Plant Species:
Integrating Experimental and Modelling Approaches," Journal of Ecology 100,
no. 1 (2011): 184–95.

A Proposal on Cedar Street

A single maple key arrives on the sill. That's chance
crossing the threshold with relief. First frost insists, No
way back out. And then the next night, in dreams, a silent
helicopter lands where it was never meant to go.
The mind, dappled grey, some leftover light, a safer
address for wind to whisper scripted fates, Samsara.
The little and beautiful proofs of trait convergence.
This samara: fruit wrapped in brown paper entering
the file drawers of winter. An unforeseeable
thinness: rented time, whirling, sealed with hypotheses.

BLACK-CAPPED

In memoriam Rehtaeh Parsons (1995–2013)*

Today the perfect storm is everyone taking shots
of branches covered in ice. Freshly severed limbs
strike brick, metal, glass, disconnecting us from the grid.
But it's the sockets of standing trees, the natural
unstained shades, that make me look away. I've been grieving
all there ever is to really grieve: the loss of what
we've taken for granted – sapwood, hardness, conductance,
density, the girl whose name I will best remember
by first spelling it backwards. Love, we barely make it
through the back door, and I'm pissed off again. It's all wrong.
Our collective stupidity, those damn smart squirrels
who feed on sunflower seeds put out for chickadees
in calamity. Glazed-over bark prevents eating
what's within: eggs, pupae, overwintering adults.

---

*committed suicide at the age of seventeen

Wetland

And it's just when I think I've won the staring contest,
a field of yellow-headed perennials arrives,
the impartialities of early September.
A great blue heron joins me for an afternoon drink
to say you never know who you'll meet. A welcome mat
of advancing rushes, petite spiked flowers, sexy
little numbers pollinated by good or bad breath.
I check out the sedges divided by diving ducks,
a beaver's leftover birch, striders defying edge
effects (landfill, wildness, property). I don't bother
with hip waders, mouth the redhead's first name – *Aythya*.
And exchange glances with whatever swims my way.

Resilience Experiment (It Is Becoming More Apparent)

We want a case study of distributed plots.
We want to make the methodology
easy. We want trends in abundance, to avoid dead matter.
We want to examine the potential
of species in the recovery treatment.

Researchers call for the need
for detecting critical indicator levels of a regime
shift: global initiatives. The vulnerability
of thorns. A measure of palatability. Randomization tests
of the exclosure period. Grazing intensities.
Lateral spread radiating from a functional
group or even disappearing entirely.

The primary producer demands further attention.
Future studies consist of only three tree species.
But it is becoming apparent that richness
alone may not be sufficient.

V. Chillo, M. Anand, and R.A. Ojeda, "Assessing the Use of Functional
Diversity as a Measure of Ecological Resilience in Arid Rangelands,"
Ecosystems 14, no. 7 (2011): 1168–77.

GROUNDS FOR SCULPTURE

April eleventh and we were alive with wooden
horses, stone breasts, steel champagne, Mexican gardeners
emptied wheelbarrows piled with manure to manicure
the lawn surrounding the attractions, polish it with
real red begonias, the sky was already too blue
to be true, we turned from admiration of a field
of hay planted (randomly, by the artist) with silk
poppies and eyed a couple against an unlabelled
pine having sex, but to our chagrin it was only
a complex configuration of coloured plastic
(Untitled), farther along a path lined with children
frozen in bronze conversation, there it was: an egg
at our feet, just broken, smaller than a chicken's but
larger than a quail's, it could have been a wood duck's if
there'd been a single wood duck around, we looked up, no
perch, only blue, and later came by a natural
swelling that we climbed, rolled down, and repeated until
cold hard lumps found all the architectural pressure
points: blade, clavicle, tomorrow's bruises and laundry
stains to serve as blue and green measures of the fitness
of this day, inclusive of grass, perhaps a few trees
rebuilt from the subconscious memory of forest
later we decided it was a peahen's decoy
egg, infertile, meant only to distract predators
and elsewhere would be the real brood in a depression
scraped in dirt, lined with discarded paper, begonias

If I Can Make It There

It's January and in the news, white fluff, cherry
trees flowering in Brooklyn. What to make of the changed
phenology? A closet of cuttings. Pale yellow
pages. Lignin destabilized where lines are preserved.
I follow greenhouse seeds, edit second editions
but need more breathing room, more literature review,
and better intentions. I must try to recycle
last year's unread New Yorkers. I must learn all the facts.
How in the nineteenth century Croatian cherries
were bleached with sulphur dioxide, dyed a candy red,
and soaked in sugar. I must attempt a Manhattan.
Sweet vermouth, bitters, that pitless heart at the bottom.

Botanic

Website icons indicating conditions so close
to optimal. Three-fifths of *Prunus* flashing in light
pink, their transmissions mapped with case-sensitive passwords.
Pointer finger to screen. Right there the true meaning of
temperate. Inclined planes are simple machines bursting
with fecundity. To wait any longer even
gravity shall be past its prime. The public garden
entrance tickets of no value. White clouds, lined in black.

Normality Assumption

Normality Assumption

The first plot has its apex
placed halfway between the Italian
Alps and an old peatland
in Estonia, between openness
and snags

A second plot winds
around immature specimens
lacking fruiting bodies
and reliable chemistry

A fifth plot is set on a clear plastic grid
with indeterminable
outline, dominated by cryptograms
at risk of harvest

Any prediction of debris
providing food and nesting materials
will not be verified

The last plot has not been
assigned a number
but will harbour photographs

C. Wagner, L.J. Schram, R.T. McMullin, S.L. Hunt, and M. Anand,
"Lichen Communities in Two Old-Growth Pine (Pinus) Forests,
Lichenologist 46, no. 5 (2014): 697–709.

Somewhere, a Lake

As sun heals the surface of ice, I lose my footing
on Ramsey Lake. My heel pierces the thin crust and I
recollect the depths to which light can take me. That day

the lake, soft at the centre, a wedding cake with white
shavings. Shoe to snowshoe to snow, phase transitions, tight
mid-winter molecules. Simple steps inflate hours

breaths of air, voids of green, making escape a landscape.
Somewhere, a lake is always ice-free. Even then there's
a lake effect, that cold wind travelling across warm

water bodies, producing energy, reminding
me I know the fluid three feet beneath me better
by summer sun. Like that night I took out the canoe

lips and atmosphere swelling with heat, a full August
moon burning a hole in the blinds, as I paddled to
the middle, ever expanding but with the absence

of perfect circles. Afterthoughts, the echoes of loons
the chord indefinable since points of reference
are never safe. All potential instabilities.

Tracks of red fox, more evidence of indirection,
their graceful arcs vanish before the grey horizon
or underneath a few centimetres of falling.

New snow quiets everything except flashy lures for
walleye below, who find the human-sized holes, baited
to surrender themselves to what they truly believe

is the eye of spring. Night freezes only the slightest
of wounds. Every morning the path is once again mine
to forge or forsake. There's an end in sight, a shore, with
pain before dawn, love after light, an outing of ice.

TABLE FOR ONE

Fingerling potatoes, duck fat, and profiteroles.
A stem topped with rosé, another glass of rosé.
Take note of the lighted, empty spaces. Take note of
surfaces, the grain of brand-new bamboo. Nodes provide
striped impressions, culm to culm stability, fair game.
But what divides fast from slow? Black-and-white checkerboard
floor with no pieces to play or replay. The tender
at the mahogany bar keeps shaking martinis.
For there are the good-natured, cumulative effects
– a century of growing seasons – or there is cost.
Every chair the same, every chair the same. The day's news
wafer-thin company, lamps lit at noon, a menu
for all seasons, and the papered walls, eager to please.

Sarah Said It Would Be Fun

We are dealt seven occupations, seven minor
improvements, two family members. We choose a colour.
We are sowing grains and vegetables, wooden pieces
shaped like wheat and carrots placed onto a square of field.
We collect sheep, wild boar, and cattle, in that order.
The writing desk is a minor improvement: when you
play an occupation, you may play a second one
for two food. The points accrue. I ask first to be green.

Two Jars

One jar holds Uncle Viswanathan's lime pickle. Not
really my uncle, a professor who taught social
work. A plain white label is affixed with Scotch
tape. Ingredients: limes, lime pickle spice. Uncle died
eleven months ago in the arms of his two sons,
his heart too fresh. The canoe capsized in Killarney.

I'm still eating his limes. Mother still has her mother's
who's been dead for fifteen years. Back in the day customs
officers yielded to those who crossed borders with two
yellow plastic buckets of unrecognizable
raw mango parts, fenugreek seeds, aniseed, onion
seeds, turmeric, red chili pepper, salt, and mustard
oil. Mother could haggle – *you will let me bring this in*
all I have left of her. A second jar contains chai

masala of Uncle Whatshisname who was always
drunk. Someone's second cousin who lived in New Delhi.
Mother almost sobered him up when she asked for a
few pounds of his secret mix. It's on my shelf in a
jam jar. Strawberries I don't preserve. We've still got a
few years or a hundred cupfuls – whichever comes first.

The Gallery

Was abandoned 27 years ago

Undisturbed by power, pollution,
or annual precipitation

It was based on ecological
reasoning and sensitive to removal

The failure of seeds to arrive
strengthened the canonical

Resident communities found it

Building a path
through subtropical forest,
they removed insignificant arrows
which made it less isolated

It provided relief among the small-scale
agriculture and granite outcrops

They experienced an intense range
shift in history, a five-fold decrease
in what was appropriate, a heavier
reliance on finding

M. Leithead, M. Anand, L.d.S. Duarte, and V.D. Pillar, "Causal Effects
of Latitude, Disturbance and Dispersal Limitation on Richness in a Recovering
Temperate, Subtropical and Tropical Forest," Journal of Vegetation Science 23,
no. 2 (2012): 339–51.

Held in a Fist

Mother knows silk and rice, grabs fistfuls at Fabricland
and Bulk Barn. Shouts out a name. Gives a grade. Quality
is a gold wedding set, fine filigree that speaks for

a wrinkled neck, the clink of everyday bangles,
hint of saffron in slow-cooked basmati rice pudding.
There are things we remember forever because they

existed. That orange-red, my hennaed palms, never
seen elsewhere, not in carnation, sunset, vein of rock.
See how pigmented roots and shoots entwine with

lifelines. Decorated stems, leaves, petals that evolve
into peacocks, polka-dotted paisley, checkerboards,
crescent moons, inward spirals. Gist plainly left unsaid.

Global Gap Structure

Take values from 1984.
Take from an individual snapshot.

We will see they are very good.

Create a model to assess the importance
of identity.

Green indicates.
Yellow indicates.
Red indicates a non-gap state.

Superimposed, with permission, is physical
detail. Like survival rates, degree
of crowding, branch extension, optimal
cutting, and how elements are exposed
to wind.

> A tree is struck by lightning with probability.
> This tree and the whole cluster of trees
> connected to it burn down and become empty sites.

Replace the terms *tree* and *empty*.

Edges migrate slowly. The bulging becomes more extreme. Do not respond until good accuracy is achieved. Until transition.

We will discuss this later.

C. Pagnutti, M. Azzouz, and M. Anand, "Propagation of Local Interactions Create Global Gap Structure and Dynamics in a Tropical Rainforest," *Journal of Theoretical Biology* 247, no. 1 (2007): 168–81.

PARLE-G

My maternal great-grandparents grew species of plums
and apricots I've never seen. Corn, wheat, vegetables,
buffaloes and cows for milk, donkeys to carry goods
hours to markets in Haripur to exchange for
raw sugar and dhal. Now orange loquats can be found
in boxes on Spadina. Mother picks them singly.
She snaps off the tough, leathery leaves that just add weight.

Mother and I are drinking black tea, a taste acquired
after Independence. Camellia sinensis
doesn't owe flavour to genetics. I stare hard at
the little girl's face on this yellow-and-red package
of Indian glucose cookies, their brand name pronounced
"parlez-ji" with a voice in my head, my convincing French
accent, though ji is Hindi and translates loosely to
"respected." In botany, pubescent means hairy.
But loquat leaves lose this trait before maturity.

RuBisCO

Turns out it is not a coincidence it rhymes with
Nabisco, the name of the most abundant protein

on earth. Shorthand for ribulose-1,5-bisphosphate
carboxylase-oxygenase, prepackaged but not

ready-to-eat, catalyst for sugar and other
complexes, limiting rates of conversion of light.

And so it was said a worthy successor to
Fraction 1 protein had at last come down like manna

from heaven, fixating carbon, sweetening our buds.

Twenty-Two Weeks

Nights lit up with a timer. Our programmable nests
evolving new synonyms. Spring is a thermostat,

a due date, a flutter. Some products are just simple
sums, but there is a harder green: multiplication

that fails to ripen. For now, well-bound prospectus, glow
on a branch. I read aloud and current children cheer.

"Oh, wie schön ist Panama!" A bear and a tiger
setting sail in a crate with the scent of bananas.

WILL IT?

Just as the right verb for yellow hits the throat, petals
dry up and green leaves emerge. This is March's grammar.
Inversions begging questions. Forsythia escapes

English hedgerows to write down rules in Mandarin script.
Communication is a bringing in. Rearrange
cut branches while there's hope for ornament or prayer.

Expand the vocabulary of interiors.
Enlighten the gardener's kitchen, her cloudy head.

Untitled

Irises. Six-fifty a bunch. Framed by a crystal
vase, two cups of groundwater from the Guelph-Amabel

Aquifer. Stems straight, attentive, their memory of mud
intact. Three blue tongues, a splash of correcting yellow.

Speechless, we descend into the trenches of marriage,
feet slippered, one hand grasping the cherry banister.

RHIZOME LOGIC

Rare are irises that live for years all dolled up
in deserts. Amidst Negev sand, starry annuals,

shrubs, and striated lizards, I came across a ring
of six flower heads, the original stalks a void

of former blooms. How satiny purple curls succeed:
openings so circular, equations fall apart.

Two Glasses

One soothes a dry throat, the other sheds a warming light.
I could swallow weeks whole simulating the decline

of centuries, the demise of watersheds, immersed
with a hard drive. The lexicons of lake beds level

climate, stanzas break the code of paleopollen,
a few micrometres to a few millennia.

On screen is a series of reticulate IF/THENs.

BELL CURVE

We're learning how to divide the gulls. Pinkness of leg,
thickness of beak, herring or ring-billed. The naked eye
can't tell from a distance. True things, even the matter
-of-factness of a seabird cry, have a tendency

to fly. Fine lines, first V-shaped, then imperceptible
on the horizon. We may slow down, domesticate,
adjust our binoculars, memorize the guidebooks,
move out to the coast, and still not stop novelty: white

-eyed, black-backed, yellow-footed, brown-hooded, glaucous-winged,
swallow-tailed. We're all taking this course, and we'll all get
some credit. See, it's the common that dictates the wild
undercurrents of interior, surface, or sea.

FORWARD–BACKWARD PROCEDURE

Because we simply do not have enough
information, a priori

Because no sequence is emitted, no conservative
lower bound

Because the annual cycling
might represent a recurring disturbance

Because well-known abilities
can be masked

We have no framework for dealing
with the shortcomings, the curve
as it approaches zero

There are four problems
that must be solved:
drought, power, psychology, and light

How many states should the final model have?

B.C. Tucker and M. Anand, "On the Use of Stationary versus Hidden Markov
Models to Detect Simple versus Complex Ecological Dynamics," Ecological
Modelling 185 (2005): 177–93.

FIFTY–FIFTY

Often happiness can be mistaken for phloem,
for adrenaline rushing through veins. But IF seasons
imbalance – functions and relations amiss, abstract
algebra no good for leafy mazes – THEN coin tosses
at mid-fall avoid the cold hard ground. I invented
a mantra: first retrace your steps. Break wooden rules, look
for false rings, the cleft between late and early, fun and
house. Find what's odd in litter's randomish settlements.
Deciduous differentials. An elegant proof.

Pine Plantation (An Expansion)

A sequence of international
signatures divided the vegetation

Linear combinations triggered
the formation of supplementary material

No resistance from resident
populations supported the establishment

Sieving thresholds defined resource
usage for the upper stratum

In the sequel, distant pools
stimulate compensatory mechanisms

An equivalent picture emerging
but with more room for nuclei

L.C.R. Silva and M. Anand, "Mechanisms of Araucaria (Atlantic) Forest Expansion into Southern Brazilian Grasslands," *Ecosystems* 14, no. 8 (2011): 1354–71.

Circo Massimo

The naked eye drawn to grandeur and ruin, flora
in the cracks of pillars, stone pines planted by Fascists,
the strange but familiar architecture of the Food
and Agriculture Organization at Viale
delle Terme di Caracalla. All equations
become worldly. To recover tropical forest
increase yields of sugar. Measure tree rings, two thousand
years of worthy weather, and Romans cultivating
grapes in more northern climes. Clink glasses of Chianti
for you'll have to agree: less than a degree is more
than necessary to account for new fiascos.

Thirty-two world records set within eighteen days, yet
in the grand scheme of things, evolution is a coast
that is receding. Another eye, intact, larger
than a human hand, still bleeding, washes up on
Pompano beach. Duke marine biologists take note
of bone fragments, ruling out squids, sharks, and octopi,
but not swordfish. Unsure, they place the unknown on ice.
We push ahead. Something bigger must have spat it out.

WHO? WHICH?

Quiscalus quiscula. A farmer's marketing. Spare.
Brutally honest. Little philosophy, for black

really does go with blue. A yellow eye, foraging
first the ground, then diversifying to eat the house

sparrows, salamanders, the legs of turtles, and fields
of corn and acorn. Look at their bodies, slightly stretched.

Sometimes singing. Close the rusty gate. Sometimes making
that short, harsh call: We are the Common. We are common.

THE NEW INDEX

It should have the circumference of a wild blueberry
pie, vinyl record, or hubcap of a Mercedes

truck. You have to take the cross-section, observe layers
of light and dark, dividing the years. The wide, early

phase of growth, release, or a crowded economy
where time is compressed, and we can only read backwards:

The condition of postmodernity. We want to know
from scars when every fire occurred, every

red pine seedling given a chance, a topography
of probabilities, learning, learning. Even death

has its seasons. How the bouquet they sent for your birth
dries up with sequence: hydrangea, rose, carnation.

Evan Said

In the near future we will grow food vertically.
The condo bubble in Toronto must first explode.

Suds, sofas, coffeemakers, and dreams will be mopped up.
Glass towers higher than First Canadian Place

will be filled up with light, whole wheat, and arugula.
There will be machinations of course. Like where to put

the cows. The bankers will enjoy their occupations.
And I will still want this: strangers to read these poems.

THE SWEET SMELL

It is a year of abundances. Frogs showing up
in swimming pools, lawns flooded with maple keys, poppies

we planted three years ago finally deciding
to show six of their heads. The farmer is promising

strawberries for next week and has brought some to prove it.
I vow to wake up early, to read more about ants,

their function in the life cycle of pink peonies.
I know it will be a lesson in mutualism,

in coevolution. But I don't have that much time.
I must invent an organism to open fists.

No Two Things Can Be More Equal

No Two Things Can Be More Equal

In undergrad I learned about the identity
matrix. Ones on the main diagonal and zeros
elsewhere. Anything multiplied by it is itself.

Then later, to love that way, and the definition
of Buddhist from a Tibetan girl across from me
and two bowls of steaming breakfast noodles in Lhasa.

If you are happy, I am happy. Fairly simple.
If you are happy, I am happy. Although was I?

Accountants would count and distribute joy if they could.
But it's simpler. Two lines of one length, parallel.

Alienation (The Transferring of Title or of Interest)

Accounts were ignition sources
from within their own perimeter,
but in recent months, climate
without change reduced
the spread of public attention

A media agent increased persistence
but there were no linkages
between abatement and refugia

Personal communication
and park status dropped
below natural levels

The lawsuit may have referred to
the next largest remnant, properties
sorted by size, scattered matrices,
the formation of a complex,
as well as the countless gaps

Criterion A: the wood turtle
taken on a voluntary basis

Criterion B: the two-lined salamander
plotted as two single bars

M. Anand, M. Leithead, L.C.R. Silva, C. Wagner, M.W. Ashiq, J. Cecile,
I. Drobyshev, Y. Bergeron, A. Das, and C. Bulger, "The Scientific Value of the
Largest Remaining Old-Growth Red Pine Forests in North America,"
Biodiversity and Conservation 22, no. 8 (2013): 1847–61.

Moving On

It takes all the running you can do, to keep in the same place.
– Lewis Carroll, *Through the Looking-Glass*

Temporal stability of sites estimated by a modified, reciprocal coefficient of variation.
– From a Ph.D.-in-progress supervisory committee meeting (2014)

I'm on a stationary bike looking at numbers.
Heart rate, calories consumed, distance travelled, time spent,
instantaneous speed. Each motivates, differently.
Health. Weight. Destination. When will I be done with this?
How am I doing? I've been obsessed with averages.
But now small fluctuations of speed don't correlate
exactly with my heart. Variation! How neurons
fire with this song. How the mind goes places. How one thigh
takes the lead, so cycles are never perfect. How with time
small deviations accumulate from sensitive
dependence on initial conditions. Then chaos.
By half the year's end I'm not where I thought I would be.

TYPE ONE ERROR

I avoid news, talk to strangers, walk around the block
a thousand times and toss nickels for random samples.
I still get a few false positives. I'm fine. It's good.
That in reality I should have ordered the eggs
Benedict. "Straw" yellow would bring out the living room
walls more than two coats of "Hay Stack." Nowadays red pines
of southern Ontario are planted, which makes seasons
easier to approximate. Even-aged stands seen
at high speeds through the window are good experience
but will not supply the needed degrees of freedom.
One deterministic seed, the mind recounting when
counting is not enough, though where many poems begin.

THE ORIGIN OF ORANGE

Elemental analyses of the orange paint
showed that it contains particles largely made up
of sulphur and arsenic. This is how Dutch masters
rendered an orange. When does metaphor appear in
the fossil record? New worlds invented the common
orange lichen, Xanthoria parietina,
long before angiosperms. Foreign fruit inspired
Old World palates. We renamed our palette. But for things
resembling a still and studied life, metaphor
fails. Hoping for sempiternal beauty, Linnaeus
quoted Pliny on Bellis perennis. Now Daisy finds
herself as we find her: picking small star-shaped flowers
of family Asteraceae, sipping orange
pekoe year after year. Waiting for a renaissance.

Cellulose and Pigment

Fresh imprints. Wet, dry, frozen days encoded in curves.
Elliptic, large-lobed, fine-toothed edges, margins predict
every unshaded niche in the disordered array
of green. Chiffon, georgette, and crepe. Shapeless beginnings.

Dozens of saris in Cellophane, missing their falls,
the amorphous blouse piece still attached, haggled over
in Chandni Chowk and Karol Bagh markets. Mother's stained
kameez. Zardozi, Kundan, Dabka embroideries

simulate flowers and future translations. Reams of
sequined silk to unravel: worm, tree, daughter, untold
like stubborn fold lines – where no light enters – and colour
fails. A lack of heritable terminology.

Tulipa 'Apeldoorn's Elite' (Darwin Hybrid)

Must not wear black to a wedding.

                And white is reserved

for funerals. Even good genes

                will not hide this shade

and immaculate blooms will not hide

                a sheltered life.

IRIS GERMANICA

Vol de Nuit, Bombay Sapphire, ras el hanout
The scent of the root is not the scent of the flower

A lack of bulbs, sword-like leaves, and yellow-bearded blooms
The name of the root is not the name of the flower

Infants may chew their hard fibrous rhizomes to cut new teeth
The price of the root is not the price of the flower

PAPAVER RHOEAS

Poppies, coquelicots, from the tamarisk- and reed-lined
roadsides of La Camargue to the heat of Marseille. Red
light, translucent petals roughened by breath alone.
Yes, this is a love affair. Yes, pharmaceutical.
For we are so often speaking of the same species.

Garam Masala

Some species cross oceans to germinate in pressure
cookers or undergraduate textbooks. They're mixed in

known parts for generating heat. Others populate
the Red List: Salim Ali's fruit bat, Nilgiri leaf

monkey, Nicobar tree shrew. Close-packing of equal
spheres. Like spices in round tiffins. Gauss proved the highest

average density, the greatest fraction of space
in infinite regular arrangement, is constant.

DERIVATION

The municipality has a scanning tool
for scrutinizing ideas

Amplified spectra show 60,000 particles,
seedlings, images, patches, species,
periods, communities, and cells

The municipality has argued
there exist thresholds
in processes, limits, rules, changes,
trends, patterns, dimensions, indicators, and structures

There exists also a unit
that measures the presence
of small degrees of concentration
of Eden

The box-counting method has obvious logistic limitations

The software generating birches, maple, and poplar
is mainly for illustrative purposes

Y. Zhang, K. Ma, M. Anand, and B. Fu, "Multifractal Pattern and Process During
a Recent Period of Forest Expansion in a Temperate Mountainous Region of
China," Ecological Informatics 6, no. 6 (2011): 384–90.

OTROS PÁJAROS

At the Universidad del Valle, in a long
fluorescent-lit room lined with cabinets to the ceiling,
Carla pulls open at thigh-height a charm of humming.
Birds sorted small to smaller. In each drawer, numbered
beaks, a new species. Andean emerald, bronzy

inca, shades only seen in silk saris or at the
cosmetics counter. Sapphire-bellied, turquoise-throated
heart hovering in mid-air. *La vida dibuja
un pájaro* (life draws a bird) *y la muerte de
inmediato dibuja otro pájaro.*

ARTICHAUTS FARCIS

Light is never still enough, has a mortifying
effect. We know how to fill but not refill. Red's wave
nanometres too lengthy to embody defeat.

I can't find that photo taken near your house in the
Camargue. Three black pomegranates split and sagging like
burst balloons. My *nature morte* hung high against white sky,
leafless grey branches. Snapped and stored only to recall

what's gone – a walk along the rice paddy, rosemary-
scented palms, *fleur de sel* from the *étang*, Provençale
artichokes from the market in Arles, a flamingo's
mating dance behind eyelids. Such predictable pink.

The World Is Charged

After Gerard Manley Hopkins

Deep Down Things

Closeted Kit Kats and Sweet Maries. Tissue paper
in Oxford shirts. Blue silk scarf worn as a tie. Argyle.
Condensed matter. Covalent bonds. Continental drifts.
Past participles. Sir John. An Invisible Hand.

The Brown Brink Eastward

Sticks of sugar cane are on sale this week at FreshCo.
Distant Indian accents command me to suck out
juice. "Never anything so sweet." But there's more than one
way to get a pulse – radial, carotid, orange
lentils in the pressure cooker, thump-thump of rolling
pin shaping a chapati. I comparison-shop.
I know the price per pound of cherries will be reduced.

The Black West

Google-Earthed the discounted green Eramosa belt
to find many-a-baubled lot. Can't zoom in but see
right there new cedar shingles, the hardened teasel, springs
beneath shale, bubbles from a nascent world, thickened lines.

The Strategy of the Majority

The Strategy of the Majority

is falling
back, pre-existing tendencies, cooperation
from the public, a vector for the spread
of catastrophic programs

purchasing strength, payoff
or penalty, the rich
are unfinished

do not bring education campaigns, economic
incentives, or ordinary
differential equations with fixed
carrying capacity
to the final destination

the strategy of the majority
is falling, reducing adherence
to control measures

the price of finding equilibria is increasing

LA Barlow, J. Cecile, C.T. Bauch, and M. Anand, "Modelling Interactions between Forest Pest Invasions and Human Decisions Regarding Firewood Transport Restrictions," PLoS ONE 9, no. 4 (2014): e90511. doi:10.1371/journal.pone.0090511.

What to Wear

At the forested foothills of the Himalayas
you touched my emerald ring to praise my hand.
Meanwhile, on the rooftops of the world
prayers were being flagged: Radha

and Krishna made an appearance in tea leaves.
A thousand singing voices were heard at once.
Recipes began to fall from inside sleeves.
Poetry was in the corridor, orchards

were full of chocolate heartwood dangling candy oranges.
Children touched stars reflected by the ocean.

There is still desire when the atmosphere becomes thin.
A lust for yak tongue, a thirst for coral.

○

I do not want settings
I want you the way
a gold border wants
a red silk sari
I want you to be the blouse
tailored to my breasts, fastened
from behind by your eyes
I do not need you under my skin
but next to my body
challenging my nakedness – I want to wear
you to the wedding party and to bed
to undress tradition

FRAGMENTATION

Brown-and-red
corridors of smocking
severing a landscape

cream crêpe de Chine
creased by forty-five
Canadian winters

my mother's hands
were taught at youth
to sew without patterns

now invented flowers
spring up between folds
and fingers

a newborn's frock
from scraps of a maiden
bedspread, new threads

embroidered at the cuffs
and hems of wedding
night henna, botanical designs

perfected by generations
to prove the worth
of every good bride

BRASSICA JUNCEA

marks the start

yellow for spring
Punjabi fields

Indian mustard
mustard   greens
Chinese   mustard
leaf   mustard

suspended in oil
and oil's promise – the hiss

of frying, mouths watering
skirts twirling – in the pressed hope

fields past, the future

tiny brown seeds

Three Laws of Physics

Orange also contains natural
and artificial orange flavours FD&C Yellow #6
wild berry also contains
artificial wild berry flavour FD&C Blue #1

Two glasses sit side by side
on the table like windows
one filled with sunshine
one with melting ice caps

No fountain, no verdant
noun and come October
the fallen light will seek
a new name (copper-like)

Shiny swirls in puddles on the driveway
take me to eleventh grade and my first close reading
of Hopkins for Ms. Korczak – *the ooze of oil*
Crushed meant childhood rainbows, our beige Pontiac
Parisienne cruising the suburb, my knees
before the accidental scrapes, thighs
before the accidental burns. That was enlightenment
right there, that old woman smelling of salami and mustard
first thing in the morning, probably coffee and cigarettes,
telling the class I was *onto something*. I still can't define poetry,
or God, but my five-year-old is wildfire when I tell her God is
everywhere. You mean in the rain? Yes. On the sidewalk? Yes.
In worms? Yes. In poo-poo? Yes.

Successional Correspondence

Management is not essential
for assessing the visible areas first

Biotic enhancements
in the face of invasion

Vascular intervention
in the face of degradation

We do not thrive
in the open

Summer may act
as a nurse, reconstructing
canonical human needs

But ecologists
recommend sowing
while the ground is covered
in snow

B. Rayfield, M. Anand, and S. Laurence, "Assessing Simple Versus Complex
Restoration Strategies for Industrially Disturbed Forests," *Restoration Ecology* 13,
no. 4 (2005): 638–49.

Nature Morte with Zoology Professor

          Spring rain spots the driveway and morning
          is delayed as

23 earthworms

          get added to the bait collection
          alongside a bucket of minnows,

55 fish

          reserved for catching bigger fish. Jean kills

2 birds

          with one stone, feeds his minnows leftover dog
          food. Speaking of birds he's once seen a chipmunk
          eat a dead bird's brain, 34 per cent unsaturated fat: who
          needs nuts? Speaking of brains his colleague
          had to shoot a video to prove that squirrels predate
          on hares, snapping off the heads of

10 small rabbits

          in one go to eat the brains, caloric equivalent
          of a winter's stash or a month's lesson
          in foraging theory.

1 man

          is going fishing today to forget about brains,
          casting bated lines

EMERGING, INFECTIOUS

In memoriam Professor Anwar Maun (1935–2007)

At Pinery Provincial Park pulling marram grass.
Beneath the dune, a network of stems connecting what
seems separate. Your fingers gently stroke the shallow
roots and bare the first lesson. From the shore, move inland.

Crest and trough, our warp and weft rewinding centuries.
A new ending, a temperate forest, black and red
oak trees mating to lose their identities. Salt still
on tongues, we contemplate the laws of gravity, grain.

Predators are removed. Herbivore populations
explode, then eat at greener beauty. Killing is cause
or effect. We cannot blame the white-tailed deer, the deer

tick, the deer tick bacterium. The final lesson
a contagion. Your body washed by your two sons, then wrapped
in clean white sheets arranged in a white pine box, forest.

GREY IS ITS OWN COMPLEMENT

The way negligee really did mean
neglected. Blues haunting
her of late: a harvest table's milk
paint, watery landscapes formed by the advances
and retreats of garage doors, the fenders
on her four-year-old's SuperCycle MoonRider.
She stood corrected in the front garden. The city came
to remove lead piping, last year's tulips
were reshuffled. She admired the two black
walnuts the grey squirrels planted,
their catholic nature, how their juglone-laced
exudate choked out flimsy periwinkle,
transparent hydrangea.

PICASSO'S GOAT

Art is a lie that makes us realize the truth.
– Pablo Picasso

Art is the lie, a female enlarging
one hundred times before laying eggs.
The truth being children

of Connecticut were getting arthritis.
Through suitable footwear, rising pant legs,
art is the lie, a female enlarging

and aspiring to deer habitat, limes, though alas it is
bacterial species, a fever, medicinal dregs.
The truth being children.

It reeks of escapement, detritus,
a million ticks, safety nets, and muskegs.
Art is the lie, a female enlarging

until water breaks, eddies toward the slightest
dependence, a bite that begs.
The truth being children.

For it's a disease of the bleak and the mightiest.
An era of victims hanging on pegs.
Art is the lie, a female, enlarging
the truth, being children.

VALEDICTIONS FORBIDDING MOURNING

After Adrienne Rich, after John Donne

Sitting crisscross-applesauce
my children count
chocolate chip cookies to be sacrificed

How they translate *Aparigraha*
with their half-Indian, half-German
tongues: non-grasping

Mamma kept telling the fable
of the brainy monkey, the greedy crocodile,
and the sweetest mangoes

I kept asking, as the tendril
asks, for nothing
but to end where it begins

Conditional B

IF The absolute difference == What's here and what was not THEN

>A confluence with climate change. From southern Texas
>red admiral butterflies arrive a month early

ELSE

>I must find that three-dollar
>net from Simply Wonderful
>before she's lost interest in entrapment

ENDIF

DO WHILE Children aren't surprised by knowledge, only visits

>It's like this: we're near the start of a game of Memory
>First she flips over a daisy and an orchid
>On her next turn she flips the same daisy
>and searches its match anew

LOOP

Power Outage

After Xi Chuan

Get it through your bright head

IF These lines == Nowhere to hang THEN

> The cut-up forests were proven to cause the floods

ELSE

> I say it another way. The birds
> you know the ones that are always singing
> pink noise? Those birds that, when you squint,
> become the blackened-in circles of tea
> –tee–tah–tah–tee–tee–tee–tee–tah?
> Those birds have nowhere to perch!

END IF

DO WHILE No trees == No lines

> You may begin your search for matches

LOOP

END

Thoughts at Crawford Lake on a Sunday Afternoon While Trying to Conceive (The Varve Is a Rhythmite)

Some strata never intermix.
Watch a meromictic lake become clairvoyant.
The absence of oxygen is a metaphor.

Corn pollen at a certain depth uncover
a local ruin. Birch bark is both flammable and buoyant.
Some strata never intermix.

Oil is neutral and water is water.
Trailed loop logic is an antidepressant.
The absence of oxygen is a metaphor.

Iroquoian longhouses, a blue-spotted salamander,
and an environmental impact assessment consultant.
Some strata never intermix.

The red herring "... lays its eggs in the nest of other ..."
"... eats small mammals like mice." Here is a white elephant.
The absence of oxygen is a metaphor.

Smoke cures every flesh including our
own. What is ours to mourn? A failed conjugant.
Some strata never intermix.
The absence of oxygen is a metaphor.

HEX CODES

Selected salmon
off the shore of Norway
will be deported

to the Pacific coast
and taught to forget
colour, season, habitat

Blackfly, mayfly, stonefly
become delicacies while fry
are dyed by numbers

Selected paint chips
from the SalmoFan™'s
palette of pinks

⬡

Consider the incensed air
of the camphor tree, born in Borneo
with Aussie lumber destiny

Animals get addicted
to its narcotic berries,
spreading invasions

until the rose-crowned fruit
dove arrives, entire rainforest
in his gut, a patch coloured in

between the eyes –
hex code #FC0FC0 –
Shocking Pink

Emerald-green canopy
of a café patio, no cell,
a napkin bleeds black ink

Buenos Aires: It is *what it is*
Dark brown remains
in tiny white cups

Windfall, sweat of September,
flowery massacre, the boulevard
coated with Hibiscus

MEAN FIELD

Let go of the ordinary
handheld calculations
of birth and death rates

You are the search for certainty
the strange attractor
grasping at panic grass

You must move
or be moved for every particle
holds its ground

Let yourself be touched by mathematical
roots, handwoven theories
fibrous and irrational

Watch spikelets think
you're some new
kind wind

THIS IS THE RING OF SIX

wedded years, gifts of sugar or iron
children, around the rosie
Number Six Cylons
species, of the genus *Quiscalus*
degrees of separation
ounces of sugar in the "easy chocolate cake" recipe
months, we spent trying to conceive
irises, connected by rhizomes
legs, of insects, breaking down macromolecules into simple sugars
hair trends to try in 2013
planets, orbited by one or more satellites
nations, of the Grand River First Nation
kingdoms, of life
poppy heads we planted three years ago, finally emerging
plastic pop yokes that have become marine litter
carbons: cyclohexane
carbons: benzene, a resonance structure

Empty Calories

aspartame

d-galactose

d-glucose

d-mannose

d-xylose

deoxyribose

dextrose

erythritol

fructose

galactose

glucose

glycerone

glycolaldehyde

isomalt

l-glucose

lactose

maltitol

maltose

polyols

ribose

saccharin

sorbitol

stevia

sucralose

sucrose

xylitol

A census of alternations, annuli, offspring

The simple beneficial, effective statistical, genetic theoretical,
a general lack of tropical, effective computational, future
empirical, last initial, periodic critical, the incorporated
individual, conservative optimal, negative additional, ballistic
several, explosive exponential, underestimated ecological

We do not aggregate

We assume all are equal

M. Anand and A. Langille, "A Model-Based Method for Estimating Effective
Dispersal Distance in Tropical Plant Populations," Theoretical Population
Biology 77, no. 4 (2010): 219–26.

NOTES

The poems footnoted with one of my scientific articles are composed solely from words and phrases found in those articles.

The majority of the poems in this book are written in 13-syllable lines. Of the three naturally occurring forms of carbon, only those with atomic mass 12 and 13 are stable, and they occur in a proportion of 99:1, respectively, in the natural world.

"The Chipping and the Tree" is for Angeline.

"We're Not Worried": The italicized lines are adapted from an article by Susan Burton in *New York Magazine* entitled "Chemistry in a Cone."

"Sarah Said It Would be Fun" is after the board game Agricola.

"RuBisCO": The quoted lines are from "Along the Trail from Fraction I Protein to Rubisco (ribulose bisphosphate carboxylase-oxygenase)" by Sam G. Wildman, *Photosynthesis Research* 73 (2002): 243–50.

"The Origin of Orange": The first few italicized words are from *Still Lifes: Techniques and Style: An Examination of Paintings from the Rijksmuseum*, edited by Arie Wallert (Amsterdam: B.V. Waanders Uitgeverij, 2000). *Geoluhread* is Old English for the colour orange, and was used until the English-speaking world was exposed to the fruit (via France) sometime in the sixteenth century. The modern colour name comes from the fruit name, originally a Sanskrit word, because the fruit has origins in Southeast Asia.

"Otros Pájaros": The quoted lines are from "La vida dibuja un árbol" ("Life Draws a Tree") by Roberto Juarroz.

"Three Laws of Physics": The first part is a found poem, from a box of Pediatric Electrolyte Freezer Pops to Prevent Dehydration. FD&C stands for Food, Drug, and Cosmetic.

"Nature Is Never Spent": The title and quoted text are from the poem "God's Grandeur" by Gerard Manley Hopkins.

"This Is the Ring of Six" is for dee.

Acknowledgements

I am indebted to the creative writing programs and communities that supported me. Here they are in roughly reverse chronological order: the Sage Hill Writing Experience (mentor: Don McKay), Creative Writing at Guelph (mentor: Paul Vermeersch), the Toronto New School of Writing (mentor: Phil Hall), U.S. 1 Poets' Cooperative (Princeton, N.J.), Banff International Research Station (Creative Writing in Mathematics and Science workshop organizers and participants), the Banff Centre Wired Writing Studio (mentor: Elizabeth Philips), the Writer-in-Residence program at the University of Guelph (particularly Jane Urquhart, Larissa Lai, and Christopher Dewdney), the Humber College School for Writers (mentors: Olive Senior and D.M. Thomas), and Eden Mills Writers' Festival (Fringe).

As a scientist I have had the privilege of working with many brilliant and creative colleagues and students (too many to name here) who provided encouragement and inspiration. I am thankful in particular for my Ph.D. supervisor, Professor László Orlóci, who insisted that I publish the first few (unpublishable!) poems I ever wrote within the pages of my Ph.D. thesis (*Towards a Unifying Theory of Vegetation Dynamics*, University of Western Ontario, 1997). I also thank my advisory and examination committee members for being open-minded enough to let them stay.

Several individuals agreed to read and critique my poems. They provided a lifeline for this book and in return asked only for friendship: Norman Cheadle, Elizabeth Socolow, Richard Sanger, and Ljiljana Coklin.

Paul Vermeersch and Noelle Allen provided invaluable encouragement on an earlier version of this manuscript. Paul provided generous feedback, for which I am forever grateful.

Earlier versions of some of the poems published here have appeared in Literary Review of Canada, Lemon Hound, The Awl, Guelph Mercury, Room, CV2, Maple Tree Literary Supplement, U.S. 1 Worksheets (Princeton), Interim, Grain, The New Quarterly, Vallum, The Shape of Content: Creative Writing in Mathematics and Science, Our Lakes Shall Set Us Free, and Spirit of the Red Pine: Art to Save the Old-Growth Forests of Wolf Lake. Thank you to the editors of these publications for including them.

I acknowledge financial support from the Ontario Arts Council (Writers' Reserve grants; recommenders: The New Quarterly, Wolsak & Wynn, Brick Books, and Diaspora Dialogues), and the Canada Council for the Arts (Grants for Professional Writers).

The School of Environmental Sciences (Ontario Agricultural College), the Ontario Veterinary College, and the College of Arts, all at the University of Guelph, and the Musagetes Foundation supported this work indirectly by sponsoring reading events in which I took part.

I am grateful to the fine people at M&S for making the book a reality and in particular to poetry board member Dionne Brand for editorial mastery bordering on wizardry.

Finally, this book would not be possible without the all-encompassing support of my husband (and friend and collaborator and brilliant scientist), my children, my parents, my siblings, and family-like friends. Thank you for your love.